Judy Blishen Soto is a California Native American who lived in Paradise, California, until November 8, 2018, when a wildfire swept through the town, destroying most of it. She had to relocate, but still lives in northern California in a town close by. Her first book was published in February 2024 about a family dog, named Tuk. This encouraged her to write another book for children aimed at conservation and teaching responsibility for the future of the earth in story form.

I dedicate my book to the people of Paradise and the clean-up crews that took all the debris away and made our town look less apocalyptic. Also, all the fire crew who helped us escape and saved many lives. The list is too long to tell you of all the help around the world that we received. Thank you all again.

Judy Blishen Soto

POEMS OF THE FIRE

Book of the Poems

AUSTIN MACAULEY PUBLISHERS®

LONDON * CAMBRIDGE * NEW YORK * SHARJAH

Ordering Information
Quantity sales: Special discounts are available on quantity purchases by corporations, associations, and others. For details, contact the publisher at the address below.

Publisher's Cataloging-in-Publication data
Soto, Judy Blishen
Poems of the Fire

ISBN 9798891558496 (Paperback)
ISBN 9798891558502 (ePub e-book)

www.austinmacauley.com/us

First Published 2024
Austin Macauley Publishers LLC
40 Wall Street, 33rd Floor, Suite 3302
New York, NY 10005
USA

mail-usa@austinmacauley.com
+1 (646) 5125767

I would like to thank my dear friend, Wanda Rold, for all the help she provided when I needed it, with re-writing and editing where it was needed, she is a computer wizard. I have learned a lot just knowing her. Thank you to the employees at Austin Macauley Publishers and the staff who made this book possible.

Table of Contents

Foreword

To whom it may concern: My story

I lived in Paradise, California for fourteen years. With only a moment's notice, I had to flee for my life. No place to go, everything is on fire. I am retired and on Social Security. I was very active in my community, singing and entertaining at senior living facilities, to supplement my income. I was also a singer for the Butte County Scottish Society in a band called The Jolly Beggers Pipes and Drums. All the music I used at my gigs was destroyed.

I was renting my home but did not have renter's insurance. I left in a panic with just the clothes on my back. Red darkened skies were unpredictable and scary. My front steps were missing as new ones were being built. It was very hard to think what to take with me. My mind went blank as I loaded the front door landing with a few things, with no steps to walk down. My home was a two-story, so I left through the garage door. That took a lot longer. I called my good friend and her words were just get into your car, stay calm and go to your cousins in Marysville. Those words stayed with me as I drove to Clark Road to descend down to the valley floor. People were still obeying the stoplights. So I was able to go right onto Clark Road. The trail of tears caught up to me and behind me, bumper to bumper. I called my cousins Jim and Brenda and asked if I could come there and they said yes. It took hours to get anywhere. I knew my life would never be the same as I knew it.

I could see the skies getting blacker and wondered how all these cars will get to safety when we're not even moving. This all happened on November 8th, 2018, a day I'll never forget. After so many hours just sitting still, windows rolled up and the air conditioner on, I was able to breathe even with having asthma. Finally, the road started to clear, but not the air. Everyone seemed to want to go to Chico, but I was headed in the other direction. With no one on the road except me, I'm home-free. I am with my family, happy and safe. I stayed with them for two months. I was lost, not knowing what happened to my friends, and the help that was available to me being so far away. So, finally, I drove to Chico to get help from FEMA and my car broke down. It saved me from the fire, but now it needed maintenance.

I remember looking forward to Thanksgiving with my family and friends and singing Christmas carols at Atria Retirement Home at the end of the month. Today is November 17th, I finally saw what was left of my home on 5513 Paloma Avenue, where my life went up in smoke and my memories are now ashes. I never gave up hope that maybe my house was spared, but that was not the case. On December 12th, a Wednesday, my friend took me to see what was left for the first time, since I received the bad news that it was gone. I found a few things on the ground like the pedals to my square piano from Vienna, it was an 1876 antique. I had to leave my second car, a 1979, 450 SL Mercedes Classic behind because the top was down and no time to put it up because it takes two people. So I laid the keys on the front seat and said I'm sorry I have to leave you behind in order to breathe. That was sad to see it burnt beyond recognition. I did find the turkey that was frozen in the freezer, cooked to perfection, that did bring a chuckle or two to my face. I asked my friend, Janet, just to be funny, if she wanted a leg or a thigh. We both laughed amid the tears. That is my story as I lived it, now is the recovery. Judith Soto.

Through The Tears

Through the tears comes cleansing
Walk out of the fire and smoke
To clear skies and see the vision
And the miracles waiting for you

10/09/2019 J. Soto

Lock Down

Lockdown
No-rebound
Ashes falling like rain
Blood moon
Cloudy skies
Smoke filled air
It hurts my eyes
No one in sight
It's all because of fright
Come to our rescue
No firemen in sight
They can't reach us
Trying with all their might
The day looks like night
All the trees are black
Lord, bring torrential rain
And put this fire out

10/10/2019 J. Soto

I'm Looking for Blue Skies

I'm looking for blue skies
Nowhere to be found
Red and black is all around
So dark nothing can be found
I call your name
Wait for you to answer
No voice returns

I pray for rain to put out the fire
Not one drop falls
It doesn't care what I desire

I plead for the wind to stop
Blowing embers all over me
I brush them off and run to safety
But none can be found
I'm just looking for blue skies
Then I will be safe and sound

10/10/2019 J. Soto

Dark Night of My Soul

When the curtain goes down
Your eyes close
Darkness takes over
No light coming through
What is happening

I can't breathe
Where is everyone
Could this be the "Dark Night of My Soul"
I have so much to do
My life is not to be shortened
And taken away because
Of the intervention of a tragedy

10/12/2019 J. Soto

I Ask You Once

I ask you once,
I ask you twice.
Once, will you help,
Twice I ask, is begging.

I have my pride,
You must know my need.
I ask once, you don't hear me,
I ask twice, you think I'm begging.

You must know my need,
By the rags I wear and the tin cup I hold,
That says please feed me.
I'll only ask once, I won't ask twice.

10/12/2019 J. Soto

No Place to Go

No place to go
The house is gone
The air is black
The ground is polluted
Everything I owned
Went up in smoke
My memories are all in ashes
All that remains is in my mind
I play the film over and over
So I can see everything again
I go back before the fire
I walk from room to room
Cherishing all that I see
I took for granted
I know where everything is
If only I could turn back time
Have one more chance, one hour,
To go back inside and gather
The things I love the most
Those precious things
I can never replace
I was happy there
But I can never walk
Through my house again
Ashes to ashes it's gone

10/25/2019 J. Soto

I Dare to Hope

I dare to hope my home was saved
I even saw it still standing
It was weeks of hoping and imagining
I revisited it many times
I walked up the steps
Put the key in the lock
Opened the door and walked in
It was so quiet and it smelled of smoke
I continued to walk and look at everything I left behind
It was still there, I picked up my albums of days gone by
If only I had taken you to my car,
In my fury for survival
My music, my precious things I could not live without
I relive that morning, with one chance to get out
What should I take, what can I live without
My heart beating, and time is running out
I only have two arms, but my mind says,
Leave it behind, the fire will die out
Your life is more important
Get in your car, run for your life
These things you possess, can't take the place
If you lose your hope to live
They can all be replaced
I dare to hope I am right

10/25/2019 J. Soto

When Tragedy Happens

When tragedy happens
Everybody becomes equal
We all know each other
Say "Hello" and smile
No more than that
We didn't have time to talk
With so many things to do in life

We all knew each other's strife
But didn't want to talk about it
It had nothing to do with our life
Move on, get things done
No time for even chewing gum

We say, "Let's get together
for lunch sometime"
But sometime never comes
Until the dark scary morning
That looked like night
All you could hear was tick-tock
The clock on the wall
Time is running out
We had so much time
Now hardly time to get out

I see these so-called friends
After the devastation
Walking on the street, so forlorn
Looking for food to eat
A blanket to keep warm

I stop to say "Hello"
I put my arms around them
They begin to cry
Oh, why didn't we take the time
When we had so much of it

We can't let go of each other
The tears and the sobbing won't stop
The ache and pain of it all won't subside
We wipe our tears and I say "I love you"
This is not goodbye

10/27/2019 J. Soto

The Night Before

As I sit here contemplating where I've been
How far I've come
I go back to the night before it happened
Not knowing the fate of my town

I was happy, content,
Enjoying all that I possessed
Sitting on my deck looking out at the trees
How beautiful it was to me

Little did I know, in the morning
All that I had would be gone up in smoke,
Fire all around me

What would I have done different that night
If only I knew

A year later today, everything is as if
Nothing happened
The red sky replaced by blue
We are celebrating our lives today
The joy of it all
Giving thanks that we are still alive
If I only knew the night before

11/8/2019 J. Soto

Falling Tears

Falling tears,
Will I ever get over you?
Where do I go to cry?
Can you hear my tears falling
Splashing on the ground.

If you could, would you comfort me?
I'm so tired of crying over
what I lost.
My life and all that was in it.

Come and comfort me.
Let us live the rest of our time together.
It's not too late.
We were in the beginning,
Let's be in our ending.

11/22/2019 J. Soto

I Cry

I cry as much when I'm happy,
As I do when I'm sad
Happy things choke me up
With emotion

11/2019 J. Soto

The Life We Had

The life we had, I feel so bad
What we lost is sad.
The fire took everything.
It showed no mercy.

November 8, 2018, was to live or die
I want to live, I cried,
Stuck on the hills of Paradise
I cry, flames nipping at my heels
Run run, said the voice inside
I pray out loud, Oh God, spare me
I don't want to die.

He heard my prayers,
That's why you're reading
These words today.

11/29/2019 J. Soto

Waves

Life is like the waves
Crashing against the shore
Knocking me to and fro
I will dive deep under the tide
Flowing back and forth
Till it throws me on the shore
I will never give up
In the eye of any storm

12/24/2019 J. Soto

Imagine

I will allow myself to dream again
Imagine life with all the things I want
I will see what gets my attention
Finding what's right for me

I'll think outside the box
Let the creative juices flow
Turn myself into a new me
Experience life as it should be

I will even take on a new persona
My face in the mirror, not like me
Even my demeanor is not who I want to be

People will wonder where I have gone,
"Not far," I say "I am here, I know where I belong."

12/24/2019 J. Soto

Learning To Just Be

I am where I'm supposed to be
There is no other place to go for me
I must be content to just be
All the bees are buzzing
Around in my head

I have to learn to just be
Until the doors open, to fly again
Then the direction will come to me

I cannot move into my new home
Unless it has been built
I cannot drive my new car
Unless I buy one

Where is my patience
To wait and just be
It's like a bowl of jello
You have to wait until it's set
Oh content for now I should be
Maybe you can help me, God

For now to just "be"

3/27/2020 J. Soto

You Can't Keep a Good Town Down

You can't keep a good town down
Even when it's burnt to the ground
We're all coming home to take
Our town, "Paradise", back
We've been through it all
We're still standing tall
The fire will never win,
Even in the wind
The people say,
You can't keep a good town down

8/31/2020 J. Soto

Lost and Confused

I'm on my way home,
Lost and confused.
I don't recognize anything.
Keep driving, something will show up.

I just crossed a bridge.
I've never driven across before.
The Police pull me over,
In my confusion I say,

"Officer, please don't arrest me,
I have a cake in the oven,
My headlights aren't working,
And I need to use the bathroom."
With that, the officer released me.
On the road again, I just passed a cemetery
It was an old cemetery
I saw a lot of cars, but no people.

I turned my headlights on,
It was a black funeral going on,
With hardly any flowers or any people.
Not even a priest did they have.
I turned the car around to go home.

I woke up in my bed,
It was a dream going on.
I close my eyes again,
I'm still lost and confused.
It's not Paradise any more.

10/2020 J. Soto

I Called 911

I called 911 to speak to Jesus,
I told Him I was in deep despair
Jesus answered and said
What's wrong my child, I can help you,
Whatever is wrong, I can make it right
Just come to me and sing me a song,
A melody that warms the heart
Music notes that ring softly in my ears
I'll fix all your problems
And make you brand new
I'll bring you a better tomorrow.

1/27/2021 J. Soto

Heavenly Town

Paradise was not just the name of a town
It was truly a heavenly experience
So close to heaven you could touch the sky

Sometimes you could ride on the clouds
and look over the town
It was a sight to behold

Sitting on top of a mountain
The view was breathtaking, even the birds
Would survey the town as they flew by

As I gazed at the beautiful view of Paradise
An angel soared close to me
I thought to myself, God must be close by

3/27/2021 J. Soto

Things Are Going to Get Better

Don't worry my friend
The past is behind us
You'll get to sing this song
You gotta be strong
Nothing lasts forever

You gotta move on
I know you're sad and dreary
Crying all the time
There is no denying
Your pain will soon be gone

The sky is blue
The grass is green
You're still standing
Because you're strong
Things are going to get better
Just hum and sing along
This sad feeling will soon be gone

8/12/2021 J. Soto

I Don't Want to Leave

I just want to stay in Paradise.
I'm tired and alone.
The fire has done me in
And I don't want to roam.
I know there is more to life,
But I just can't keep going,
All I want to do is just stay in my home.

5/21/2021 J. Soto

Episodes

Episodes in my life,
Beginning, middle, ending.
Enjoy it before it comes to an end.
Give me one more drag off my cigarette
And one more sip from my drink.

5/21/2021 J. Soto

California Goin'

Goin', California goin' down the hill
People are leaving, nowhere to go
Can't afford rent or food
What are we goin' to do
Earthquakes a shaking,
Temperatures are rising
Too hot, we are all burning,
No electricity, can't breathe,
No breeze, ocean a dying,
No fish in the sea,
Only garbage and debris
We destroyed our world
What are we going to do
Can't turn back the clock
To make it stop.
Poor men are rich now.
Rich men leaving the high-rises
Homeless living high, and taking
Their place, no more on the ground,
Businesses going out of business
Shops shutting down
Can't afford to make a living,
This country is goin' down,
Say goodbye to California
Someone is responsible,
Bring back the life we used to have
We want to feel safe and sound.

6/21/2021 J. SOTO

It Pays to Pray

My worries are few because
My blessings are more
I'm so grateful to God
For all his love, I thank him everyday
When I count my blessings one by one
It always pays to pray

7/2021 J. Soto

The Void

There will be a void in my life without you
You were a special person to me
A void is where you once stood
The memories of your long life,
All that you were, I will always remember.

I will miss you so,
but treasure all the good times we shared,
While you were here on this earth
No one can ever replace the special person
you became
I will close my eyes and bring you back, In my mind, with all the memories
you gave me,
I will see you once again embedded in my
Thoughts forever.

7/2022 J. Soto

Today

God led me in the direction I should go
We don't have time under our circumstances
Rise above your circumstances
It will change soon, tap into God's power

You'll never change what you tolerate.
Believe, be aggressive,
You'll have the devil in a phone booth
Dialing 911

Walk with authority,
Put a spring in your step

God can breathe life into your finances
God will take you places
You've never been before.
God is God of the beautiful

God is behind me, wherever I go
I will not live in fear.

7/2022 J. Soto

Maui on Fire

A reminder of what fire can do
The Lush Island of Lahaina, Maui, is gone
On August 8th, 2023
Burnt to the ground
It brings back the memory
of the Paradise fire, November 8, 2018
The worst fire in the U.S. History
It has surpassed the Paradise toll
Red Cross, Samaritan's Purse, volunteers
Everyone, all called to help
The Maui people had no warning
The fire caused by a hurricane
Knocking down power poles
Causing explosions and fire everywhere
No place to go, except to run for your life
Straight to the Oceans waters, but,
The ocean is raging too,
Destructive waves
It's do or die, they just want to cry
"Help"
Another Paradise gone

8/8/2023 J. Soto

In Your Storms

I hold you strong in your storms
You are secure in my arms
The winds can blow and howl
Even beat you to the ground
My presence protects you
I am the "Great I Am"
In the midst of it all, I am with you
You may feel the wind
You may hear the thunder
See the darkness and the rain
I shall cover and protect you
With my love I surround you
Remember my promise
Just know, I'll never let you face your
Storms alone, I hold you strong and make
a promise they will pass
The light will turn on again
I have full rein over the rain
I am always with you
In all your "STORMS"

8/11/2023 J. Soto

Still Waiting

The fire in Paradise has been over for five years
Some of us are still waiting for Fire Money
With nothing to live on
Some money came to some and some it did not
Meeting after meeting, letter after letter
PG&E said, "Please be patient, it's coming"

Our Patience is running out
The people we're staying with,
our welcome has run out

We don't have possessions like we used to
From a hoarder to a minimalist
A few treasures to remember who we were
Our spirits are dropping rapidly
Below coping
We're trying to hang on to their promises
That's all that keeps us going
Another phone call
Another promise
We're still waiting

8/11/2023 J. Soto

In My Room

Sitting in my room, that's all I have,
A bed, a dresser and a desk,
A few pictures on the wall.
After the fire, that's all.
A guitar, I never play,
It sits against the wall.

I take to my writing,
Drift off into another world.
Where I leave my room,
For a little while.

Creating music, songs, stories,
Escaping what my life has become
And wonder what it will be,
If I broaden my horizons.

3/09/2024 J. Soto

Epilogue
My Life After the Fire

It was like being reborn again. I came into the world with nothing, everything I had in my life took sixty-plus years to build and now the smallest items, like underwear to a toothbrush, hairbrush and a plastic bag to put them in.

My friends were all spread out everywhere, displaced. I don't know where they are, any place they could find shelter. My support group gone, no one to comfort me.

I lost my beautiful home with all my treasures in it. The flair I had for decorating, the clothes and gowns I wore for entertaining, theater, plays, and singing. All my poems and stories I wrote, were getting ready to put in a book, to be published. Family albums, and movies of my life – all irreplaceable. Artwork and portraits are gone.

Now I know how homeless people feel; being homeless has a new meaning for me. Looking for a place to shower, a towel to dry off, where to use a bathroom, toilet paper is not to be found. I soon realized no one wants to let a homeless person use their bathroom. My new home is in my car for now. I called my cousin in Marysville, and they invited me to stay with them for a while.

How? At the last portion of my life, which took a lifetime to build, can I do this again? I find myself without a job, a home, to have any energy to rebuild. Now all I can get are the basics to survive, to replace the lifestyle I had in my retirement years, I don't think that I have the energy I had when I was younger to do this again.

Two years later, I still do not have a place of my own. I am staying with a friend, who also lost their home. A room and a bath, rules and regulations, even with that I am grateful. No music or singing in the places our friends used to get together to sing and dance, at Smokey Mountain Steakhouse and Italian Gardens on Skyway in Paradise, they both burnt to the ground.

I lost the musical part of my life, with no piano allowed in the house, my life is silent now. My asthma has made it harder to breathe from all the smoke

I breathed from the Campfire. My car that I drove out of the fire also needed repair, from all the ash and smoke, trying to get out of Paradise. With many repairs to get it running again. So I was without a car until I could get some extra money for repairs. I left my Mercedes convertible behind because I needed to breathe and took the other car with air conditioning.

With each day that goes by, I remember in my mind, the belongings I had. Is there enough time to replace everything I had, and feel the joy of having a home of my own again?

Revisiting the day of the fire, November 8th, 2018, therapy sessions, looking for help from FEMA, Camp Wildfire Assistance Program and friends, I don't look the same, feel the same, dress the same or breathe the same. I hope I haven't shortened my life by this tragedy. Now at last, but not least, I am in lockdown because of Covid 19, which magnifies everything, I am now just trying to stay alive so I can live again.